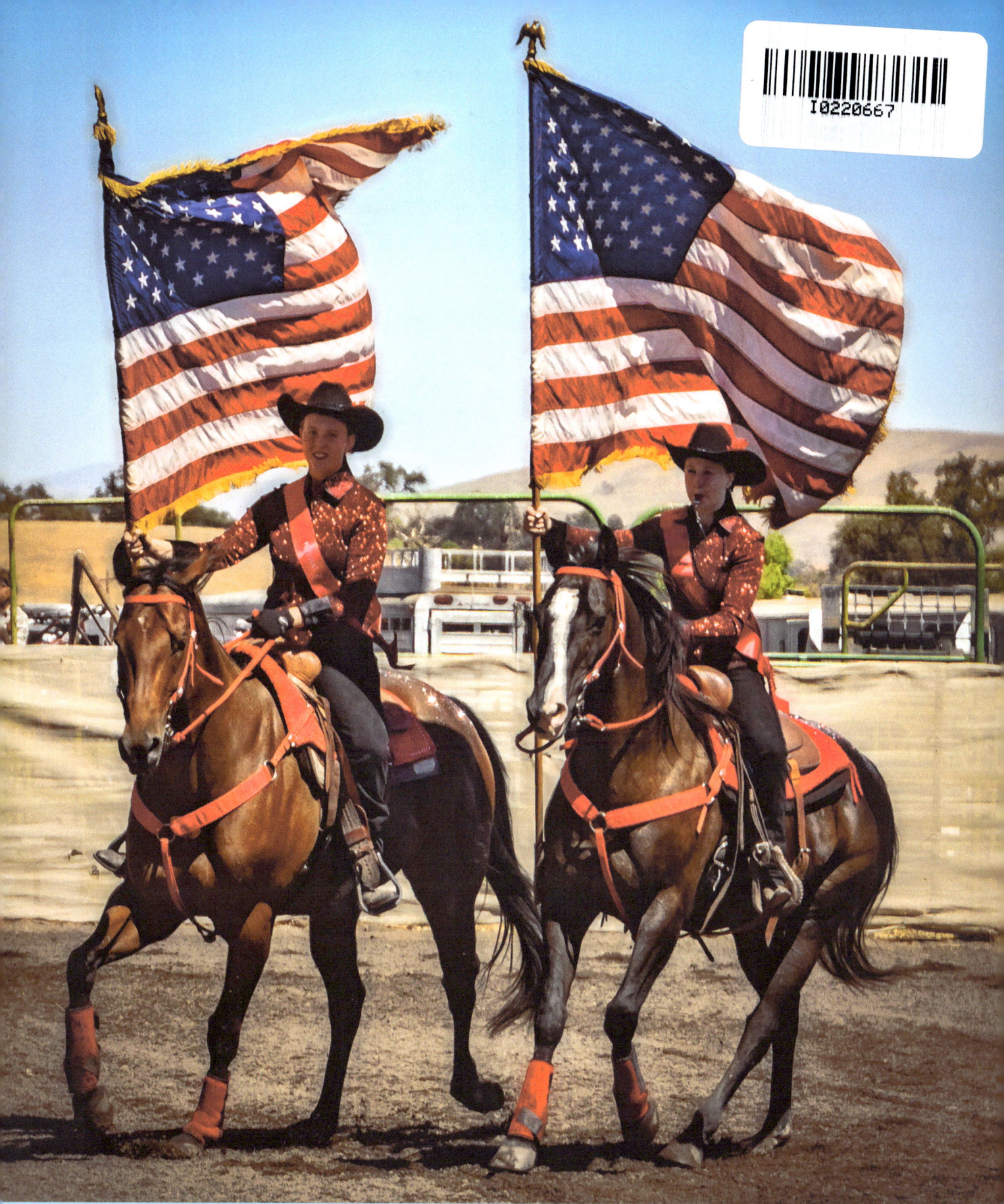

Creston Rodeo Impressions:
skill, family, friendship,tradition, exitement, and fun.

CRESTON RODEO IMPRESSIONS
skill, family, friendship, tradition, excitement, and fun.

Published by Sharing Magic Moments, 451 Lancaster St., Cambria CA 93428
Visit ElisabethHaug.com,
Contact: Info@EHaug.com

Photographed and written by Elisabeth Haug
ISBN: 978-0-9662715-3-9
Nature/Animals/Horses and Nonfiction > Photography > Photo-essays & Documentaries

OTHER BOOKS BY ELISABETH HAUG:

Heaven on Earth: Horses in California Sand and Surf ISBN: 781729380406
Das Islandpferd ISBN 1981675574
New Age Vikings: There is Something About The Icelandic Horse ISBN 145639852
New Age Vikings, the Icelandic Horse. Volume One ISBN 0966271553
New Age Vikings Volume 2, Horsegathering in Iceland ISBN 0966271521
In the Hoofprints of the Vikings, Horse Trekking in Iceland ISBN 0966271505
Eldhestar: fun, wide vision, and adventure ISBN 1461094836
Dogs Just Wanna have Fun ISBN-0982606400
California Elephant Seals ISBN 0982606486
Cambria A Modern Camelot ISBN 154316061
Morro Bay: A Magical Marriage of Man Made and Nature ISBN 1545566240
Motion Is Emotion: Action Photography Unleashed ISBN 0966271599
A Finger on the Shutter 0966271513
The Legend of God and Pegasus ISBN 0966271884
Horse Trekking in Iceland: the ultimate adventure.

It is a given, that most horse oriented San Luis Obispo County residents look forward to the yearly Creston Classic Rodeo. It takes place in September and is family oriented and a great spectator event—friendly, fun, skillful, and exiting.

My aim with this book is to share my magic moments at the rodeo over the last four years. Because I expect my pictures to speak for themselves, my book relies on photos rather than text to tell the story.

The first Creston Rodeo took place in 1996 as a fundraiser. The goal was to contribute towards building a community and recreational center in the small village of Creston. Nowadays higher education scholarships are offered to worthy applicants.

The first Creston Rodeo took place in 1996 as a fundraiser. The goal was to contribute towards building a community and recreational center in the small village of Creston. Nowadays higher education scholarships are offered to worthy applicants.

The event has become extremely popular with California cowboys and cowgirls as well as riders from other states.

The rodeo takes place each year in September. It is a lively three day event filled with community participation. It succeeds in displaying both the spirit of the modern and the old west.

The rodeo is community staffed and organized. It has a relaxed, happy atmosphere nd preserves the legacy of the steadfast pioneers that settled the area.

Some of the classes offered at the rodeo are barrel racing, mutton bustin', ribbon roping, team roping, steer stopping, sort and rope, ladies breakaway, ribbon roping, hide race, steer riding, tie down roping, ribbon doggin, sort and brand, and double mugging.

"Bull riding may be dumb but it's fun"

"Get on, Ride hard, Hold nothing back, and give it all you've got!
Thats the Cowboy Way!!!"

May your belly never grumble, may your heart never ache, may your horse never stumble, may your cinch never break

Winning ain't everything but losing ain't fun either. Ride to win!!

If you haven't fallen off a horse...
then you haven't been riding long enough.

A cowboy doesn't ride a bull for fame,
he rides because he loves riding.

Cowboys have a way of looking at things a little differently than the rest of us.
Their wisdom is simpler and more down to Earth.

When you lose, don't lose the lesson.

"A cowboy is a man with guts and a horse."
– William James

Cowboys have a way of looking at things a little differently than the rest of us.
Their wisdom is simpler and more down to Earth.

When you lose, don't lose the lesson.

"A cowboy is a man with guts and a horse."
– William James

Do not go where the path may lead,
go instead where there is no path and leave a trail.

About Me—
The Photographer/Author:

I love life—horses, photography, dogs, people, other animals, nature, and clear communication.

My mission is to share my magic moments. My favorite way of doing so is through photography.

Mine is a "one stop photography shop". I am available for photo shoots, photography lessons, and workshops. And I sell photo downloads, prints, greeting cards, photo books and gifts. I also edit photographs on demand and assist people with their websites and social media. I create books, flyers, and other marketing media for horse businesses, and have created and published 12 photo books

I have bred and trained Icelandic Horses for the better part of a life time. I feel this helps me greatly in my horse photography, especially so, when action is involved. Understanding horses as well as riding, and having watched horses over the ages enables me to understand and predict movement, to be precise, and to be fast enough on the trigger to catch the peak moments.

My family and I came to California on Thanksgiving Day in1978 bringing with us a plane load of Icelandic Horses.

Drawn by the wide open spaces and the pioneer spirit of the area, we bought a ranch close to Creston and settled there. Later—for business reasons—I moved on to the Santa Ynez Valley. I wantd to capitalize on the Scandinavia heritage of the area. But, now, I am back to living in San Luis Obispo Count, and have made Cambria my home..

To view more of my photography and to learn more about my services, check out my website at ElisabethHaug.com and my Facebook pages Elisabeth Haug's Photoart and Elisabeth Haug's Horse and Pet Photography.

Contact me at info@ehaug.com or at (760)805-8651

Some of the 2018 Creston Rodeo sponsors were:

Rodeo Benefactor: Brian Pritt
Best Ever Saddles/ Ryan & Tammy White
Premier Ag / Glen & Annie McWilliams
Resistol Hats / Dustin Noblitt
Rohrer Hay and Feed / Linda Rohrer
Shadle Insurance / Jon & Elizabeth Shadle
Southwest Fence and Supply/ Chris & Monique Hanneken
805 / Matt Malone
Mazzi Tank Co. / Billy Franz
Outback Internet LLC / John Rees
Plasvacc USA Inc. / Heather Alspach
Arrogant Bastard Ranch / Stephen Bruce
American Riviera Bank/ Ann Hansen
Aptos Smoke Tree LLC/ Mike and Hilde Romelfanger
Arrogant Bastard Ranch / Stephen Bruce
C & N Tractors / Jeff Sponhaltz
CalPortland Construction / Doyle Davis
Boot Barn/ Trigg Garner
Farm Credit West / Dave Bedell
J B Dewar Inc. / Ken Dewar
KC Feeds/ Cecil Martinez
KPRL-AM 1230 / Kevin Will
Mid-State Solid Waste and Recycling / North County Recycling / Brad Goodrow
Nutrien Ag Solutions/ Darin Chabot
Paso Robles Equine/ Colter Negranti
Platinum Properties / Cindy Petrovich
Robert Lewis
San Luis Sports Therapy / Jason Roda
Stephen Hovey Accountancy Corp. / Stephen Hovey
Umpqua Bank / Katie Crocker
West Coast Auto & Towing / Gil Luera
Whitaker Construction / Tony & Amy Lewis
Wildwind Manor/ Oksana Tovt
Pamela Pierson / Mike Young
2D Ryan Ranch/ Noel & Nancy Ryan
Bernard Ranch/ Ron & Becky Bernard
Browder Painting Company / Ryan & Jennifer Browder
Central Coast Propane / Brent Wingett
Chandler Ranch / Linda Wood
Coast Pipe / Kris Broucaret
Creston News / Ann Spencer

Duane Baxley Cattle Co. / Duane Baxley
Equine & Canine News / Nola Johnson
Farm Supply / Pam Pickering
Filipponi & Thompson Drilling / Ned Thompson
G. Wiemann Construction Inc. / Greg Wiemann
John Whitford Communications / John Whitford
La Panza Ranch / Stacey Twisselman
Mark's Tire Service / Lisa Jennings
Mike Cole Farms/ Mike Cole
Navajo Rock and Sand/ Judy Lewis
Pacific Premier Bank / Deanna Elmerick
Paso Robles Pioneer Day Committee / Shan McCornack
Pauly Trucking/ Chris Pauly
Rabobank / Anna Hoffman
Ray M. Buban Financial & Tax Services / Ray Buban
R S Inspection / Ray & Susan Smith
Shadow Run Vineyards & Winery / Les Evans
The Metal Shed / Bruce & Rosie Hebron
The Watergap Saver/ Mike & Terrie Estrada
Tierrsanta d'Olivas / Les & Debbie
Bob & Donna Giubbini
John & Diane Evangelista
Kevin Matea
Bernice Raymond
Gay Molina
Idlers Home / Jennifer Idler
The Metal Shed / Bruce & Rosie Hebron
Western Janitor Supply Inc. / Linda Buss
Dave Christy

www.ingramcontent.com/pod-product-compliance
Lightning Source LLC
Chambersburg PA
CBHW042016080426
42735CB00002B/77